THE CLOCK

Richard and Louise Spilsbury

Heinemann
LIBRARY

Chicago, Illinois

www.heinemannraintree.com
Visit our website to find out more information about Heinemann-Raintree books.

To order:

☎ Phone 888-454-2279

🖥 Visit www.heinemannraintree.com to browse our catalog and order online.

Edited by Louise Galpine and Laura Knowles
Designed by Philippa Jenkins
Original illustrations © Capstone Global Library
   Limited 2012
Picture research by Mica Brancic
Originated by Capstone Global Library Limited
Printed and bound in China by CTPS

15 14 13 12 11
10 9 8 7 6 5 4 3 2 1

Library of Congress Cataloging-in-Publication Data
Spilsbury, Richard, 1963-
  The clock / Richard and Louise Spilsbury.
    p. cm.—(Tales of invention)
  Includes bibliographical references and index.
  ISBN 978-1-4329-4877-1 (hc)—ISBN 978-1-4329-4886-3 (pb) 1. Clocks and watches—Juvenile literature.
I. Spilsbury, Louise. II. Title.
  TS542.5.S67 2012
  681.1'13—dc22   2010036494

Acknowledgments
We would like to thank the following for permission to reproduce photographs: Alamy pp. **6** (© Tony Lilley); Corbis pp. **13** (Reuters/© Stephen Hird), **15** (© Stefano Bianchetti); Getty Images pp. **5** (Julian Herbert), **8** (Time & Life Pictures/Dmitri Kessel), **17** (Science & Society Picture Library), **18** (Hulton Archive), **20** (Science & Society Picture Library), **24** (Science & Society Picture Library), **25** (Photographer's Choice/ Michael Dunning), **26** (AFP Photo/Carl Court); Mary Evans Picture Library pp. **9**, **21**; Rex Features p. **19** (Alisdair Macdonald); Science Photo Library p. **22** (Sheila Terry); Shutterstock pp. **4** (Mosista Pambudi), **11** (Vaclav Hajduch), **23** (© Germany Feng); The Bridgeman Art Library p. **10** (British Library, London, UK/© British Library Board. All Rights Reserved).

Cover photograph of large electric clocks being carried into a factory in London, England, in 1936 reproduced with permission of Corbis/© Hulton-Deutsch Collection.

We would like to thank Peter Smithurst for his invaluable help in the preparation of this book.

Every effort has been made to contact copyright holders of material reproduced in this book. Any omissions will be rectified in subsequent printings if notice is given to the publisher.

Disclaimer
All the Internet addresses (URLs) given in this book were valid at the time of going to press. However, due to the dynamic nature of the Internet, some addresses may have changed, or sites may have changed or ceased to exist since publication. While the author and publisher regret any inconvenience this may cause readers, no responsibility for any such changes can be accepted by either the author or the publisher.

CONTENTS

Look for these boxes ●

Biographies

These boxes tell you about the life of inventors, the dates when they lived, and their important discoveries.

Setbacks

Here we tell you about the experiments that didn't work, the failures, and the accidents.

EUREKA!

These boxes tell you about important events and discoveries, and what inspired them.

Any words appearing in the text in bold, **like this**, are explained in the glossary.

TIMELINE

● **2011**—The timeline shows you when important discoveries and inventions were made.

A HISTORY OF TELLING TIME

Up until about 6,000 years ago, most people were farmers. Many lived in different places throughout the year, hunting for food or moving their livestock to areas with enough food. There was no need to tell time, because life depended on natural cycles, such as the changing seasons or sunrise and sunset.

Gradually, more people started to live in larger settlements, and some needed to tell time. For example, priests wanted to know when to carry out religious ceremonies. This was when people first invented clocks—devices that show, measure, and keep track of passing time. Clocks have been important ever since. Today, clocks are used for important things such as setting busy airport schedules.

Knowing when to pick crops at their best depends on the weather, but telling time helps people plan when to sow seeds and harvest.

4

around 4000 BCE—
The earliest city, Eridu, is built in the Middle East

around 3500 BCE—
People use shadow sticks as sundials to measure time (see page 6)

Inventing clocks

There are many different kinds of clock today, from clocks that can time races down to thousandths of a second, to clocks that tell you the exact time on the other side of the world. As with most other important inventions, the clock wasn't thought up by one person all at once. The invention of the clocks we use today involved many inventors and inventions along the way.

In 2002 Americans Daniel Rogacki and Francis Graney invented an underwater pace clock. This was for swimmers to check their training times without stopping to look at a pool clock.

Racing against the clock! Athletes use extremely accurate clocks to time races.

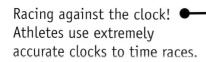

5

EARLY TIME TECHNOLOGY

Sundials were the first real timepieces. Sundials show the time of day by the position and length of a shadow cast by the Sun. Early people noticed that a shadow cast by a tree was long in the morning, and then grew shorter and shorter until it disappeared at midday, when the Sun was overhead. Then it grew longer again, on the other side of the tree, toward nightfall. The first sundials were sticks in the ground with marks or stones around them to show where the shadow fell at regular intervals.

EUREKA!

From about 3500 BCE, Egyptians built tall stone **obelisks** at the entrances to temples. Ancient Roman invaders of Egypt took obelisks back to Rome to show off their victories. Some obelisks were then used as public sundials!

This Egyptian obelisk was brought to Rome around 2,000 years ago.

around 1500 BCE—A water clock is placed in Egyptian **pharaoh** Amenhotep I's tomb (see page 8)

2000 BCE   1000 BCE

How do sundials work?

Viewed from Earth, the Sun appears to change position in the sky throughout the day. The Sun shines on a sundial from a different height and angle each hour. This makes the sundial's shadow change position, too. However, it is Earth that is moving, not the Sun. Like a ball with a stick through it, Earth spins around its **axis**. This is a slightly slanted imaginary line that goes through Earth from pole to pole. Earth takes 24 hours to spin around once. When one side of Earth faces the Sun, it is daytime there. When it faces away from the Sun, it is night.

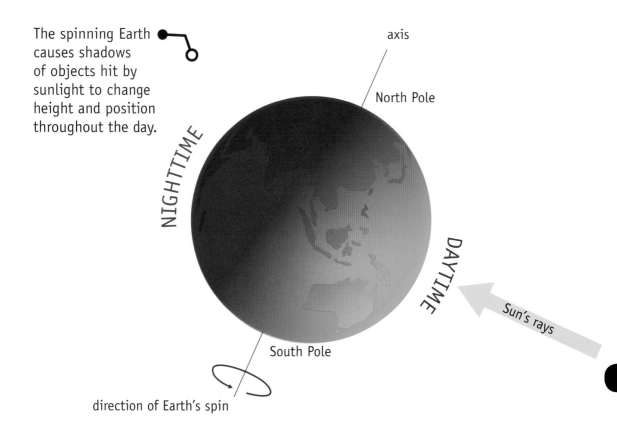

The spinning Earth causes shadows of objects hit by sunlight to change height and position throughout the day.

axis

North Pole

NIGHTTIME

DAYTIME

Sun's rays

South Pole

direction of Earth's spin

around 255 BCE—An improved *clepsydra*, or water clock, is invented in Greece (see page 9)

1200s CE—Monks use early mechanical clocks (see page 10)

0

1000

Changing levels

A big drawback with sundials is that they do not work at night! People invented other ways to measure time. In early water and sand clocks, water or sand passed out of a small hole in one container into another below it. A scale marked on the inside of the lower container showed time by how much it had filled up. One of the oldest water clocks was found in the tomb of the Egyptian **pharaoh** Amenhotep I, who was buried around 1500 BCE.

Clay water clocks such as this were used in ancient Greece. Often they were used to measure the length of speeches.

around 1510—Peter Henlein invents the first spring-powered clock (see page 16)

Water thieves!

A major problem with water clocks was that as the water in the upper bowl ran out, the water flow got slower. This was because there was less **water pressure** bearing down. In ancient Greece, water clocks were called *clepsydras*, meaning "water thief." Greek inventor Ctesibius came up with a *clepsydra* that remained the most accurate clock for hundreds of years. In his clock, water dripped at a constant rate and raised a float. This pushed up a bar that moved a pointer around a dial to show the time.

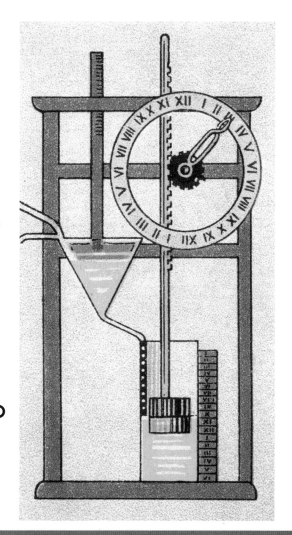

The large dial on this *clepsydra* is different from the ones on clocks today. Can you see how?

Ctesibius (around 285–222 BCE)

Ctesibius was a barber, but he preferred inventing objects, such as an adjustable mirror to make cutting hair easier! He became a famous mathematician and inventor, and he invented new machines such as an air-powered catapult, a water pump, and the *clepsydra*.

THE FIRST MECHANICAL CLOCKS

In European **monasteries** in the **Middle Ages**, monks had to pray at certain times of the day and night. When they used a water clock or burned a candle to tell the time, someone always had to stay awake to watch it. That person would then ring a bell to wake the others. By the 1200s, monks had begun to use mechanical clocks powered by falling weights.

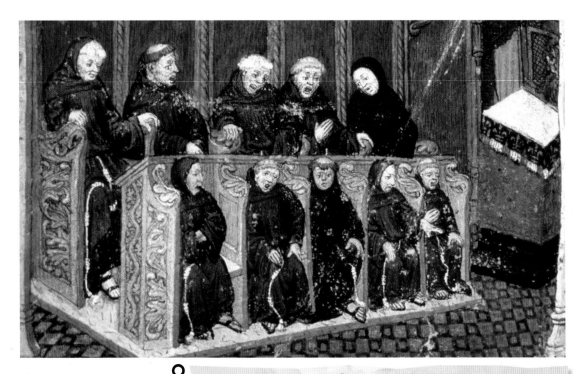

Mechanical clocks made it much easier for monks to know when to gather for their religious services.

Setbacks

Early mechanical clocks were very inaccurate and could be off by 30 minutes or more a day. Some even had to be corrected by checking them against a sundial!

1571—The first wristwatch is said to have been made for, and worn by, England's Queen Elizabeth I (see page 17)

1550   1560   1570

Falling and turning

Early mechanical clocks used **gravity**, the force that pulls objects on Earth toward the center of the planet. In early mechanical clocks, there was a weight attached to a toothed wheel, which turned as the weight fell. To make the weight fall slowly and regularly, there was a horizontal crossbar. The crossbar moved from left to right, alternately stopping and releasing the wheel, tooth by tooth. This type of control became known as the escapement.

Mechanical clocks gradually became more decorative as people added features such as moving clockwork figures.

EUREKA!

Early mechanical clocks did not have faces with dials or pointers. Instead, they simply marked the passing of time by the ringing of bells. The Latin word for bell is *cloca*, and this is where we get the word "clock" from.

1580s—Galileo Galilei discovers that pendulums swing back in perfect time, but it is many years before pendulums are used in clocks (see page 12)

1580   1590   1600

Swinging clocks

A big improvement in mechanical clocks came in 1656, when Dutch astronomer and mathematician Christiaan Huygens built the first pendulum clock. A pendulum is a weight at the end of a rod that swings back and forth at a regular speed. Huygen's clock was driven by a falling weight just like earlier clocks. But the swinging pendulum more accurately controlled the speed with which the hands turned around the clock face.

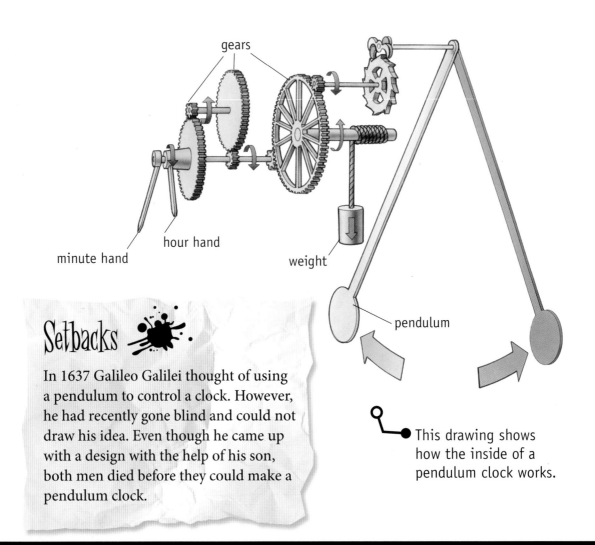

gears

hour hand

minute hand

weight

pendulum

This drawing shows how the inside of a pendulum clock works.

Setbacks

In 1637 Galileo Galilei thought of using a pendulum to control a clock. However, he had recently gone blind and could not draw his idea. Even though he came up with a design with the help of his son, both men died before they could make a pendulum clock.

Just a minute!

The pendulum was a big improvement on earlier clocks because it only varied 10 to 15 seconds a day. Most of the earlier weight-driven clocks had one hand to measure time in hours or quarter-hours. Around 1650 a minute hand was invented. Pendulum clocks were so much more accurate than earlier clocks that, by 1690, a minute hand was added to many clocks.

The giant clock tower known as Big Ben, in London, England, has a 4.4-meter- (15.4-feet-) long pendulum. It swings every 2 seconds.

13

1637—Galileo thinks of using a pendulum to control a clock

Around 1650— The minute hand is invented

1630   1640   1650

Christiaan Huygens (1629–1695)

Christiaan Huygens was born in The Hague, in the Netherlands. His father was a politician and poet and many famous poets, painters, and thinkers were guests in the family's home. Huygens was surrounded by interesting ideas from an early age. He was good at drawing and mathematics. In college, Huygens studied law as well as mathematics because it would get him a better job. However, Huygens's questioning mind soon led him to study astronomy, too.

Huygens also became an inventor, not only of clocks, but also of telescopes and a rather dangerous engine that ran on gunpowder! In 1656 Huygens was the first person to discover the true shape of the rings around the planet Saturn. He saw them while using an improved telescope he and his brother had designed. In 1673 he published a famous book called *Horologium*, which explained how to make a pendulum clock. Shortly before he died, Huygens wrote his last book, in which he wondered about the possibility of life on other planets and stars!

1656—Christiaan Huygens builds the first pendulum clock

1673—Huygens publishes *Horologium*, explaining how to make a pendulum clock

1650

1660

1670

15

1675—Huygens develops
the balance spring
(see page 16)

1680   1690   1700

PORTABLE CLOCKS

In the 1400s some wealthy people had mechanical clocks in their homes. These were big and heavy, since they had weights on long strings inside. By 1510 German lock maker Peter Henlein had invented a clock powered by winding up a coiled spring. This stores **potential energy** in the spring. As it unwinds, the spring's potential energy turns to **kinetic energy** (movement), which turns the hands of the clock. However, the hands only moved at the right speed when the spring was tight. In 1675 Christian Huygens developed the balance spring. This is a fine spiral spring that keeps clock hands moving at the same speed.

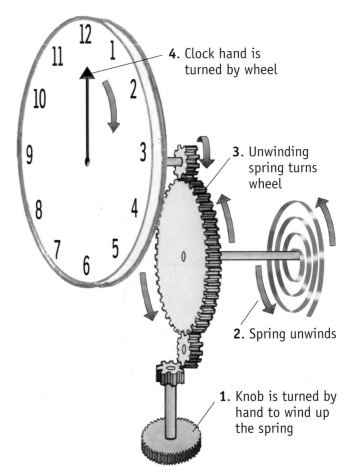

4. Clock hand is turned by wheel

3. Unwinding spring turns wheel

2. Spring unwinds

1. Knob is turned by hand to wind up the spring

Energy from the wound spring in a clock gradually turns cogs, which slowly rotate hands around the clock face.

1714—The British government offers a reward to whoever can invent a very accurate clock, called a **chronometer** (see page 19)

1700   1710   1720

The first wristwatch or "wristlet" was said to have been a gift given to England's Queen Elizabeth I in 1571. It was admired in the royal court and, over the next centuries, wristwatches became fashion accessories only for rich women.

It is difficult to tell the time using this very early pocket watch from the late 1600s.

Getting smaller

People started to make spring-powered clocks to stand on tables in their homes. They also wore them as pocket watches throughout the 1700s and 1800s. The development of railroads in the 1800s meant that people had to know the time to be able to catch a train. During the Boer War in southern Africa (1899–1902) and World War I (1914–18), attacks were carried out at particular times, and soldiers needed to know exactly when to take cover or charge forward. Soldiers found it awkward to get their pocket watches out of jacket or pants pockets, so they started wearing them on their wrist. Soon watchmakers began producing more and more wristwatches.

1735—Clockmaker John Harrison tries to make a chronometer, but it is not accurate enough (see page 19)

Clocks at sea

Earth is always spinning, so local times at different places vary. For every 15 degrees of **longitude** you travel east, time moves ahead by one hour. Going west, it moves back by one hour.

In the 1600s, sailors measured local time using the Sun's position in the sky. They compared that time to the one shown by ship clocks, which were set at the start of voyages, to figure out their longitude. The trouble was that ship clocks could not keep good time over long voyages—for example, because they were rocked on rough seas. This meant that sailors often got longitudes wrong.

In 1707 four British Royal Navy ships were wrecked on rocks off Britain's Scilly Isles, killing 2,000 men. The navy believed that a better ship clock for figuring out position might have saved them.

Loss of H.M.S. Association on the Scillies. 22. Oct. 1707.

1759—John Harrison invents a chronometer for use at sea, called the H4

1750   1760   1770

A race against time

In 1714 the British government offered a big reward to anyone who could make a very accurate clock, called a **chronometer**. British clockmaker John Harrison's first attempt in 1735—named H1—lost too much time. He then made more clocks with improvements, such as balances and springs to reduce the effects of rough seas. Harrison invented his winning chronometer, H4, in 1759.

Harrison's H4 chronometer was the most accurate clock of its day. In a two-month-long voyage from London to Jamaica, it lost only five seconds of time.

EUREKA!

With the invention of trains and steamships, people began to travel around the world much faster. Because of this, it was difficult to keep track of all the different local times. In 1884 an international conference decided to fix this by dividing the world into 24 time zones, based on their longitude. Now when we travel, we change clocks by an hour for each zone we move into.

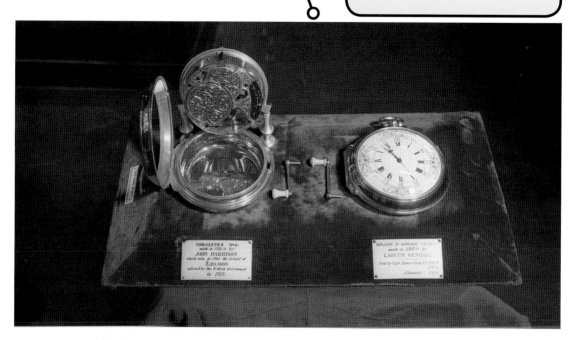

ELECTRIC CLOCKS

The problem with even the best mechanical clocks is that their springs need to be wound up or their pendulums and weights need to be repositioned to keep them working. In 1840 Scottish inventor Alexander Bain applied for a **patent** for his invention of the first clock driven by an electric motor. **Electricity** is the type of **energy** we use to power most machines. Electric clocks keep going for as long as the electricity is turned on.

Battery power

Batteries contain chemicals that react together to make electricity. Early batteries were big and unreliable, but in 1957 the Hamilton watch company sold the first electric watch. This had a small battery to keep it going without the need to be wound up.

Battery watches like these were made until 1969, when they were replaced by quartz technology (see page 22).

Alexander Bain (1811-1877)

When Alexander Bain had the idea for an electric clock, he had no money to build it. He went to scientist Charles Wheatstone for help, but instead Wheatstone advised Bain to stop work on it. Shortly after, Wheatstone made a copy of the clock and claimed it was his own invention! Luckily, Bain already had a patent—legal proof of his invention—so Wheatstone was forced to pay him a fine. This fine meant Bain could afford to set up his own business.

1840—Alexander Bain applies for a patent for his invention of a clock to run on an electric motor

Quartz clocks and watches

Early electric clocks still had pendulums or springs inside. American Warren Marrison invented a quartz clock in 1929. Quartz is a kind of **crystal** that **vibrates** at a regular rate per minute when electricity passes through it. It wasn't until 1967 that the technology was available to make small quartz clocks and watches. Quartz watches were more accurate, reliable, and eventually much cheaper to make than earlier electric ones. In today's quartz watches, electricity makes a crystal vibrate, and a **microchip** turns these vibrations into regular electric pulses that change the time.

Quartz crystals vibrate at different rates, depending on their size and shape. Most crystals used in clocks and watches look like tiny tuning forks!

Setbacks

To begin with, quartz watches were very expensive. The watch company Seiko sold the first quartz watches in 1969. But few people could buy one, as the company only made 100 and each one cost as much as a car!

Digital displays

On digital clocks, time is shown as changing numbers on a small electronic screen, instead of as moving hands on a fixed clock face. The first digital display was invented in 1968. Today's digital clocks use **LCDs**, or liquid crystal displays. When electricity passes through the special liquid in these displays, the liquid can be made to form clock numbers. These show up on the small screen.

EUREKA!

A futuristic digital clock appeared in the background of a famous 1968 movie called *2001: A Space Odyssey*. This inspired the team behind the invention of the first real digital watch!

Digital displays show 24-hour time, as well as the hours, minutes, seconds, and usually the day and date, too!

23

1884—World time zones are introduced (see page 19)

1899—People start to wear wristwatches for the first time (see page 17)

1880   1890   1900

Atomic clocks

Atomic clocks are even more accurate than quartz clocks. They only lose about one second in 30 million years! U.S. physicist Isidor Rabi first suggested using the vibrations of **atoms** to measure time in 1937. The first atomic clock was made in 1955 by British scientist Louis Essen. An atom is the smallest part of a chemical **element** that can take part in a **chemical reaction**. Inside an atomic clock, there is a cloud of atoms, usually cesium atoms. A **laser** beam passes through this cloud and counts the vibrations of the atoms. It uses these fast, regular vibrations to keep time.

Setbacks

Atomic clocks may be accurate, but most are large (at least the size of a refrigerator), heavy, very expensive, and use a lot of power.

This is the first atomic clock, *Cesium I*. Cesium atoms vibrate 9.2 billion times every second.

Why do we need atomic clocks?

You might be surprised to know that most of us use atomic clocks every day! Many phone conversations can be transmitted at the same time along the same wires. Atomic clocks control the rapid switching between speaker and listener for each conversation, to make sure the calls do not get mixed up.

Communications companies often use the atomic clocks on **Global Positioning System (GPS) satellites**. The system uses satellites in space to locate positions on Earth. A GPS unit receives signals from atomic clocks on four or more satellites out in space. The GPS measures the time differences between the signals to calculate its position and height to within a few feet.

Each of the 24 GPS satellites in space carries 4 atomic clocks.

1937—Isidor Rabi suggests using vibrations of atoms to measure time

1930   1940   1950

INTO THE FUTURE

Today, a huge variety of clocks can be used for more than simply telling the time. MP3 players have alarm clocks that can be set to wake you up to your favorite music. There are clocks set into rings that not only tell time, but also take your pulse to measure your heart rate. There are even clocks that project numbers into the sky!

Numbers were projected onto a building in London on New Year's Eve. They counted down the seconds before 2010 began.

1955—Louis Essen builds the first atomic clock (see page 24)

1957—Hamilton watch company sells the first electric watch (see page 20)

1968—The first digital display is invented (see page 23)

1950   1960   1970

EUREKA!

The H2O Multifunction Clock has a special battery that releases electrical **energy** to power the clock when it touches water. To keep the battery going, the wearer just refills it with water every few months.

Tomorrow's clocks

In the future, scientists plan to improve time technology. For example, a new generation of atomic clocks using entangled **atoms** on a **microchip** could be accurate to one second in three billion years! This level of accuracy could improve **GPS** systems on Earth and also help spaceships navigate through space to other planets.

In the future, we may even have tiny atomic clocks the size of grains of sand inside our cell phones that figure out times and locations accurately for us. We may have paper-thin clocks built into sheets of stickers. What clocks do you think inventors will create in the future?

1969—Seiko starts to sell the first quartz watches (see page 22)

2002—Rogacki and Graney invent an underwater swimming pace clock (see page 5)

1980   1990   2000

TIMELINE

around 4000
BCE
The earliest city, Eridu, is built in the Middle East

around 3500
BCE
People use shadow sticks as sundials to measure time

around 1500
BCE
A water clock is placed in Egyptian **pharaoh** Amenhotep I's tomb

1673
Huygens publishes *Horologium*, explaining how to make a pendulum clock

1656
Christiaan Huygens builds the first pendulum clock

1650
The minute hand is invented

1675
Huygens develops the balance spring to regulate a spring-driven clock

1714
The British government offers a reward to whoever can invent a very accurate clock, called a **chronometer**

1759
John Harrison invents a chronometer for use at sea, called the H4

2002
Rogacki and Graney invent an underwater swimming pace clock

1969
Seiko starts to sell the first quartz watches

1968
The first digital clock display is invented

around 255 BCE
An improved *clepsydra*, or water clock, is invented in Greece

1200s CE
Monks use early mechanical clocks

around 1510
Peter Henlein invents the first spring-driven clock

1637
Galileo Galilei thinks of using a pendulum to control a clock

1580s
Galileo Galilei discovers that pendulums swing back in perfect time

1571
The first wristwatch is said to be made for, and worn by, England's Queen Elizabeth I

1840
Alexander Bain applies for a **patent** for his invention of a clock powered by an electric motor

1884
World time zones are introduced

1899
People start to wear wristwatches for the first time

1957
The Hamilton watch company sell the first electric watch

1955
Louis Essen builds the first atomic clock

1937
Isidor Rabi suggests using vibrations of **atoms** to measure time

GLOSSARY

atom building block of all matter, it is the smallest part of any element

axis central line around which something rotates

chemical reaction when two or more substances are mixed together and change into different substances

chronometer accurate clock or watch

crystal solid substance that is made up of an ordered arrangement of atoms

electricity form of energy from the flow of an electric charge

element single chemical unit, such as hydrogen or uranium

energy form of power, such as heat, movement, or electricity

Global Positioning System (GPS) network of computers that use time signals sent to and from satellites to locate positions on Earth

gravity force of attraction between objects, especially between a very large object such as Earth and other objects near it

kinetic energy energy of movement

laser instrument that creates thin beams of high-intensity light waves

LCD stands for Liquid Crystal Display. This is a flat electronic display panel that filters light to produce an image.

longitude measurement of the position of something on Earth by how far east or west it is from a line called the Greenwich Meridian

microchip small crystal wafer that can carry out many electronic functions

Middle Ages historical period between roughly 500 and 1450 CE

monastery place where a community of monks (religious men) lives

obelisk pillar usually made of stone or concrete and used as a monument or sundial

patent official proof that an invention, idea, or process was the idea of a particular person. It protects it from being copied.

pharaoh ancient Egyptian king

potential energy stored energy—for example, in a compressed spring or a weight before it falls

satellite human-made or other object that moves in orbit around Earth or another planet

vibrate move rapidly up and down or back and forth

water pressure push of water on an object caused by its weight

FIND OUT MORE

Books

Duffy, Trent. *The Clock (Turning Point Inventions)*. New York: Atheneum, 2000.

Jenkins, Martin, and Richard Holland. *The Time Book: A Brief History from Lunar Calendars to Atomic Clocks*. Somerville Mass.: Candlewick, 2009.

Maestro, Betsy, and Giulio Maestro. *The Story of Clocks and Calendars*. New York: HarperCollins, 2004.

Mara, Wil. *The Clock (Inventions That Shaped the World)*. New York: Franklin Watts, 2005.

Raum, Elizabeth. *The Story Behind Time (True Stories)*. Chicago: Heinemann Library, 2009.

Websites

www.nist.gov/pml/general/time/index.cfm
Visit the website of the National Institute of Standards and Technology to read a fascinating history of clocks and time.

http://tycho.usno.navy.mil/cesium.html
There is a lot more information about cesium atomic clocks and how they are used on this U.S. Navy website.

Places to visit

The American Clock & Watch Museum
100 Maple Street
Bristol, Connecticut 06010
www.clockandwatchmuseum.org

The United States Naval Observatory
3450 Massachusetts Avenue, NW
Washington, D.C. 20392-5420
www.usno.navy.mil/USNO

INDEX